D0387240

MAX on life
cd-book :: study

Building a
Godly Home

4 Interactive Bible Studies
for Individuals or Small Groups

MAX LUCADO

THOMAS NELSON PUBLISHERS

Copyright © 2007 by Max Lucado

Published by Thomas Nelson, Inc., P.O. Box 141000, Nashville, Tennessee, 37214.
Study Guide prepared by the Specialty Group of Thomas Nelson, Inc.
Excerpts from *When God Whispers Your Name* and *A Love Worth Giving*,
published by W Publishing Group. Used by permission.

All rights reserved. No portion of this book may be reproduced, stored in a retrieval system, or transmitted
in any form or by any means—electronic, mechanical, photocopy, recording, or any other—except
for brief quotations in printed reviews, without the prior written permission of the publisher.

Unless otherwise marked, Scripture quotations are taken from *The Holy Bible*: New Century Version.
Copyright © 1987, 1988, 1991 by W Publishing Group, a Division of Thomas Nelson, Inc.
Used by permission. All rights reserved.

Scripture quotations marked NIV are taken from *The Holy Bible:*
New International Version (NIV). Copyright © 1973, 1978, 1984 by the International Bible Society.
Used by permission of Zondervan Publishing House. All rights reserved.

ISBN 978-1-59145-561-5
www.thomasnelson.com

CONTENTS

HOW TO USE
THIS STUDY GUIDE

Congratulations! You are making God's Word a priority. These moments of reflection will change you forever. Here are a few suggestions for you to get the most out of your individual study.

:: 1 ::

As you begin each study, pray that God will speak to you through His Word.

:: 2 ::

Read the overview to each study, then listen to the audio segment, taking notes on the worksheet provided.

:: 3 ::

Following the audio segment, respond to the personal Bible study and reflection questions. These questions are designed to take you deeper into God's Word and help you focus on God and on the theme of the study.

4

There are three types of questions used in the study. *Observation* questions focus on the basic facts: who, what, when, where, and how. *Interpretation* questions delve into the meaning of the passage. *Application* questions help you get practical: discovering the implications of the text for growing in Christ. These three keys will help you unlock the treasures of Scripture.

5

Write your answers to the questions in the spaces provided or in a personal journal. Writing brings clarity and deeper understanding of yourself and of God's Word.

6

Keep a Bible dictionary handy. Use it to look up any unfamiliar words, names, or places.

7

Have fun! Studying God's Word can bring tremendous rewards to your life. Allow the Holy Spirit to illuminate your mind to the amazing applications each study can have in your daily life. ∎

INTRODUCTION

BUILDING A GODLY HOME

A wedding is an event, but a marriage is an achievement. Marriage demands the greatest level of tenacity and talent and tenderness that any human being can summon. The odds seem stacked against its success from day one. How bizarre that two people could stand up before heaven and friends, gaze into each other's eyes, and promise to ride the roller coaster of life together. It's zany, unbelievable, and yet it's God's plan. The institution of the home is God's idea. When God saw Adam's solitary soul He went to work, creating a companion for the man. He united Adam and his mate in history's first wedding. With giraffes for bridesmaids and lions for groomsmen, the couple marched down a tree-lined aisle carpeted with pine needles. And God Himself joined the two together.

God is a covenant maker. He will help you honor yours. If you are just starting a family or if your seasoned marriage needs rebuilding, you have a God who charges you to call on Him to build the godly home He longs for you to have. ■

*Even if a marriage
is made in heaven,
man is still responsible
for the maintenance.*

DR. JAMES C. DOBSON

LESSON ONE:

WHERE ARE
WE HEADED?

Clothe yourselves with compassion, kindness, humility, gentleness and patience. Bear with each other and forgive whatever grievances you may have against one another. Forgive as the Lord forgave you. And over all these virtues put on love, which binds them all together in perfect unity.

COLOSSIANS 3:12B–14 NIV

OVERVIEW

It's easy to start out on the wrong foot, both in marriage and in travel. I did, a few years ago. I was in Portland, Maine, catching a flight to Boston. I went to the desk, checked my bag, got my ticket, and went to the gate. I went past security, took my seat, and waited for the flight to be called. I waited and waited and waited—

Finally, I went up to the desk to ask the attendant and she looked at me and said, "You're at the wrong gate."

Now, what if I'd pouted and sighed, "Well, there must not be a flight to Boston. Looks like I'm stuck."

You would have said to me, "You're not stuck. You're just at the wrong gate. Go down to the right gate and try again."

Many of us are at the *wrong gate* in our marriages and family lives. It's not too late! We simply need to find the "right gate"—and try again.

The first step to improving your relationship with your spouse and children is improving your relationship with God. When you put Him first and begin to extend His love and grace to those in your household, you'll be headed in the right direction: a household that honors God and loves each other.

PART 1:
FOLLOW-ALPHA NOTES

USE THIS WORKSHEET AS YOU LISTEN TO "BUILDING A GODLY HOME, PART 1."

- The Most Important Decision in a Marriage:

- The Most Important Foundation of a Marriage:

The secret to having _____ in marriage is understanding the

    forgiveness you have from _____.

Relationships are secured by _____ not _____.

- The burlap sack of your life:

1. The stones of rejection:

2. The stones of regret:

- Brides and grooms have high aspirations and high expectations; they bring their sacks along.

- The first step to improving your relationship with your spouse is improving your relationship with God.

Ephesians 5:28:
  The man who loves his wife loves himself.

- Accepting God's forgiveness will make you easier to live with!

PART 2:
GOING DEEPER

PERSONAL STUDY AND REFLECTION

· What is one quality or ability that you believe most sustains a marriage
relationship? Why?

_____

_____

_____

· How is that quality or ability reflected in your own home life?

_____

_____

_____

- Read Ephesians 5:22–33.

- According to verses 22 and 23, what is the relationship of the wife to the husband, and vice versa?

_____

_____

_____

_____

- How are husbands commanded to love their wives? What are wives to do in return?

_____

_____

_____

_____

- How does the bond between Christ and His Church illustrate the love of a husband for his wife?

_____

_____

_____

_____

- Why should the bond between a husband and wife be greater than the bond between a parent and a child? (See verse 31.)

_____

_____

_____

_____

- In sum, what are the responsibilities of the husband and wife toward each other? (See verse 33.)

_____

_____

_____

_____

- Why is unselfishness an essential part of a Christian marriage?

_____

_____

_____

_____

_____

· How does a healthy Christian marriage honor the Lord? Honor the
Church? Provide a witness to others?

_____

_____

_____

_____

_____

_____

_____

_____

- How can you treat your own spouse/family members with more love and respect this week?

_____

_____

_____

_____

_____

_____

_____

_____

*The greatest of all arts is
the art of living together.*

WILLIAM LYON PHELPS

LESSON TWO:

VIVE
LA DIFFERENCE!

Christ accepted you,
so you should accept each other,
which will bring glory to God.

ROMANS 15:7

OVERVIEW

My parents were not too big on restaurants. Partly because of the selection in our small town. Dairy Queen offered the gourmet selection, and everything went downhill from there. The main reason, though, was practicality. Why eat out when you can stay at home? Restaurant trips were a Sunday-only, once-or-twice-a-month event.

Every time we ate at home, my mom gave my brother and me the same instructions: "Put a little bit of everything on your plate."

We never had to be told to clean the plate. Eating volume was not a challenge. Variety was. Don't get me wrong. Mom was a good cook. But boiled okra? Asparagus? Were they really intended for human consumption? According to Mom, they were, and—according to Mom—they had to be eaten. "Eat some of everything." That was the rule in our house.

But that was not the rule at the cafeteria. On special occasions we made the forty-five minute drive to the greatest culinary innovation since the gas stove: the cafeteria line. Ah, what a fine moment indeed to take a tray and gaze down the midway at the endless options. Yes to the fried fish; no to the fried tomatoes. Yes to the pecan pie; no, no, a thousand times no to the okra and asparagus. Cafeteria lines are great.

Wouldn't it be nice if marriage were like a cafeteria line? What if you could look at the person with whom you live and select what you want and pass on what you don't? "H'm, how about a bowl of good health and good moods. But job transfers, in-laws, and laundry are not on my diet."

Wouldn't it be great if love were like a cafeteria line? It would be easier. It would be neater. It would be painless and peaceful. But you know what? It wouldn't be love. Love doesn't accept just a few things. Love is willing to accept all things—even the differences you may face in your marriage.

PART 1:
FOLLOW-ALONG NOTES

Use this worksheet as you listen to "Building a Godly Home, Part 2."

- It's very easy to miscommunicate!

- The average engaged couple spends _____ hours preparing for the wedding service and only _____ hours in premarital counseling preparing for the marriage.

GENDER ISSUES

- Men and women are different creatures!

- We are wired differently.

- Robert Cohn study on toddlers: Boys and girls have different communication styles.

- Women focus on the _____; men focus on the _____.

- What men lack in _____, they make up for in

_____.

Every couple comes with a set of rules and regulations about how to communicate.

FAMILY OF ORIGIN ISSUES

- We come from different family backgrounds.

- Learn the person to whom you are communicating.

OUR OPTIONS

- Look for greener grass.

- Settle for dead grass.

- Create new grass.

PART 2:
GOING DEEPER

PERSONAL STUDY AND REFLECTION

· Have you ever known someone who treated love like a cafeteria line? If so, how did this person treat others?

_____

_____

_____

· Read 1 Corinthians 13:4–7.

· Does the fact that love is willing to accept all things mean that love never tries to change some of those things? Explain.

_____

_____

_____

• What are some of the greatest differences between you and your spouse?

_____

_____

_____

• Which are the differences that are the hardest for you to accept? Why?

_____

_____

_____

God's view of love is like my mom's view of food. When we love someone, we take the whole package.

• What are some of the ways you try *not* to take the entire package of your spouse?

_____

_____

_____

· What part of your entire package has your spouse had a hard time
  accepting? Explain.

_____

_____

_____

_____

· In what practical ways can you begin to overcome the differences between
  you and your partner and bridge the gap with love?

_____

_____

_____

_____

- Which have you tried to do in the past: "look for greener grass"; "settle for dead grass"; or "create new grass"? Explain.

_____

_____

_____

_____

- How can you begin to create "new grass" in your marriage this week?

_____

_____

_____

_____

_____

*The Christian is supposed
to love his neighbor, and since
his wife is his nearest neighbor,
she should be his deepest love.*

MARTIN LUTHER

LESSON THREE:

RULES FOR A HEALTHY MARRIAGE

*So let us try to do
what makes peace and
helps one another.*

ROMANS 14:19

OVERVIEW

In the 1930s, Joe Wise was a young, single resident at Cook Hospital in Fort Worth, Texas. Patients called him the "doctor with the rose." He made them smile by pinning a flower from bedside bouquets on his lab coat.

Madge, however, needed more than a smile. The automobile accident had left her leg nearly severed at the knee. She was young, beautiful, and very much afraid. When Joe spotted her in the ER, he did something he'd never done before.

Joe took his lab coat, bejeweled with the rose, and placed it gently over the young woman. As she was wheeled into the operating room, the coat was removed, but she asked to keep the flower. When she awoke from surgery, it was still in her hand.

Dr. Wise didn't stop there. As Madge recovered, he paid visits to her room. Many visits. When he learned that she was engaged, he hung a "No Visitors" sign on her door so her fiancé couldn't enter. Madge didn't object. Her diary reads, "I hope that handsome young doctor comes by to visit today." He did, that day and many others, always with a rose. One a day until she was dismissed from the hospital.

And Madge never forgot. Her response? She gave him a rose in return. The next day she gave another. Then the next, another. As they started dating, the daily roses still came. When they married, she didn't stop giving them. Madge convinced the Colonial Golf Course across the street from her house to plant roses so she could give the doctor his daily gift. For nearly forty years, every day—a rose. Their younger son, Harold, says he can't remember a time when there wasn't a glass in the refrigerator containing roses for his dad.[1]

That's what keeps a marriage strong—maintaining the love you find in the beginning over the course of a lifetime. Here are some "rules" to help you do just that.

[1] My appreciation to Dr. Harold Wise and Dr. Joe Bob Wise for allowing me to tell their parents' story.

PART 1:
FOLLOW-ALONG NOTES

USE THIS WORKSHEET AS YOU LISTEN TO "BUILDING A GODLY HOME, PART 3."

- Ephesians 4:25–32

I. The Principle of _____ - _____

  • The more _____ the relationship, the more

  _____ the abuse.

  • Tell each other the truth!

  • Be able to receive the truth.

  • As long as there's secrets and silence, there's separation.

II.The Principle of _____ - _____

• You can't cash more than you deposit:

• Build up your love account by exercising kindness.

• Three phrases that will make deposits:

1. "I feel as if . . ."

2. "Let me see if I understand."

3. "I'm sorry."

   • Nurture your relationship

   • You will never forgive anyone more than God has already forgiven you.

III. The Principle of Claw-removing

   • "Never shout angrily . . ." (Ephesians 4:31).

   • You are never justified in hurting your spouse with your words.

   • You will never have to forgive your spouse more than God has already forgiven you.

PART 2:
GOING DEEPER

PERSONAL STUDY AND REFLECTION

• Which of the three rules of a healthy marriage comes the easiest for you?

_____

_____

_____

_____

• Which is the greatest challenge?

_____

_____

_____

_____

THE PRINCIPLE OF CLOAK-SHEDDING

· Read John 5:14.

· What does it mean to say that Jesus *is* the truth? How can He help bring truth to your marriage?

_____

_____

_____

· What secrets, if any, are you keeping from your spouse? Why are these truths so difficult to tell?

_____

_____

_____

· What can you do today to begin to better open the lines of communication between you and your mate?

_____

_____

_____

THE PRINCIPLE OF CARE-GIVING

· Read 1 Corinthians 13:4.

· How could more of God's love and kindness make a difference in your marriage?

_____

_____

_____

- In what ways have you recently built up your "love account"? In what ways have you depleted it?

_____

_____

_____

_____

- List three practical ways in which you could make a deposit into your love account today.

_____

_____

_____

THE PRINCIPLE OF CLAW-REMOVING

• Read James 3:1–12.

• What attitudes and emotions are most prevalent in your marriage?

_____

_____

_____

_____

• What do you tend to do when you become angry? How do you react?

_____

_____

_____

- How can you begin to react to difficult situations with more of God's love?

_____

_____

_____

_____

_____

_____

_____

_____

_____

*When home is ruled according
to God's Word, angels might be asked
to stay with us, and they would not
find themselves out of their element.*

CHARLES SPURGEON

LESSON FOUR:

THE DYSFUNCTIONAL FAMILY REUNION

It takes wisdom to have
a good family, and it takes
understanding to make it strong.

PROVERBS 24:3

OVERVIEW

My friend Mike tells how his three-year-old daughter, Rachel, lost her balance and hit her head against the corner of an electric space heater. After a short cry, she blacked out. Her parents rushed her to the hospital, where the tests revealed a skull fracture.

Pretty traumatic for a child. Pretty traumatic for Mom and Dad. Rachel was kept overnight for observation and then sent home. She spent a couple of days understandably quiet. But Mike knew she was okay the morning he heard her talking to herself. He was still in bed, and she was down the hall in her room. "Bear? Doggie? Sheep? Baby? Ruff-ruff?" Mike smiled. She was calling roll in her crib, taking inventory. After all, she'd been through quite an ordeal, and she wanted to make sure things were in order.

Suppose we follow her lead? Let's take inventory. Let's take stock of our relationships. Think for a minute about the people in your world. Aren't they valuable? Aren't they essential? Aren't those relationships worth whatever it takes to keep them healthy?

Think of it this way. When you are in the final days of your life, what will you want? When death extends its hand to you, where will you turn for comfort? Will you hug that college degree in the walnut frame? Will you ask to be carried to the garage so you can sit in your car? Will you find comfort in rereading your financial statement? Of course not. What will matter then will be people.

If those relationships will matter the most then, shouldn't they matter the most now?

So what can we do to strengthen them? Following Rachel's example would be a good start. She inventoried her hands and hair; let's take an inventory of our hearts.

How well do we love the people in our lives? Let's make sure the way we treat our families reflects the way God has treated us.

PART 1:
FOLLOW-ALONG NOTES

USE THIS WORKSHEET AS YOU LISTEN TO "BUILDING A GODLY HOME, PART 4."

- Genesis 48–50

- Joseph's family is a prime example of a dysfunctional family.

- Is there such a thing as a "functional family"?

PRINCIPLES FOR SURVIVAL
IN A DYSFUNCTIONAL FAMILY

1. Give _____ to the _____.

   • Judah repented and returned to his family.

   • Prodigals do return.

2. Give _____ to the _____.

   • Exodus 20:12

   • Have you honored your parents for what they did right?

1. Give _____ to the _____.

   • Genesis 47:27-31

   • Genesis 50:1-14

• Sometimes God blesses the many because of the faith of one.

PART 2:
GOING DEEPER

PERSONAL STUDY AND REFLECTION

· How well do you love the people in your family? Your spouse? Your children? How can you love them more the way that God loves them?

_____

_____

_____

· Read Colossians 3:18–21.

· How does this passage of Scripture describe a "functional" family? How does it compare with your own family?

_____

_____

_____

- What are the responsibilities of wives and husbands?

_____

_____

_____

- What are the responsibilities of the children?

_____

_____

_____

- How do God's instructions to families help family members become mature Christians?

_____

_____

_____

- Why should Christian parents rear their children in an atmosphere of encouragement?

_____

_____

_____

- How can they do so?

_____

_____

_____

- Which of God's principles for Christian households challenge you to change?

_____

_____

_____

- How will you do so?

_____

_____

_____

- What is one way you can improve the way you treat each member of your family?

_____

_____

_____

In your quiet time, thank God for the many ways He has blessed your home and family. Be as specific as possible, naming each individual blessing. Then ask Him to show you how you can better be a spouse and a family member who reflects His love and grace. Do not conclude your prayer until the Lord has revealed to you several ways in which you can practically share the light of His love in your family. ■

PROMISES FROM
BUILDING A GODLY HOME

Savor the following promises that God gives to those who determine to build their families on a godly foundation. One way that you can carry the message of this study with you everywhere in your heart is through the lost art of memorization. Select a few of the verses below to commit to memory.

*A man will leave his father and mother and be united
with his wife, and the two will become one body.*

GENESIS 2:24

*Wives, yield to your husbands, as you do to the Lord, because the
husband is the head of the wife, as Christ is the head of the church.
And he is the Savior of the body, which is the church. As the church yields
to Christ, so you wives should yield to your husbands in everything.
Husbands, love your wives as Christ loved the church and gave himself
for it. . . . Husbands should love their wives as they love their
own bodies. The man who loves his wife loves himself.*

EPHESIANS 5:22–25, 28

Love is patient and kind. Love is not jealous, it does not brag, and it is not proud. Love is not rude, is not selfish, and does not get upset with others. Love does not count up wrongs that have been done. Love is not happy with evil but is happy with the truth. Love patiently accepts all things. It always trusts, always hopes, and always remains strong.

1 CORINTHIANS 13:4–7

Tell each other the truth, because we all belong to each other in the same body. When you are angry, do not sin, and be sure to stop being angry before the end of the day.

EPHESIANS 4:25B–26

When you talk, do not say harmful things, but say what people need—words that will help others become stronger. . . . Do not be bitter or angry or mad. Never shout angrily or say things to hurt others. Never do anything evil. Be kind and loving to each other, and forgive each other just as God forgave you in Christ.

EPHESIANS 4:29, 31–32

Wives, yield to the authority of your husbands, because this is the right thing to do in the Lord. Husbands, love your wives and be gentle with them. Children, obey your parents in all things, because this pleases the Lord.

COLOSSIANS 3:18–20 ■

SUGGESTIONS FOR MEMBERS OF A GROUP STUDY

The Bible says that we should not forsake the assembling of ourselves together (see Hebrews 10:25). A small-group Bible study is one of the best ways to grow in your faith. As you meet together with other people, you will discover new truths about God's Word and challenge one another to greater levels of faith. The following are suggestions for you to get the most out of a small-group study of this material.

1. Come to the study prepared. Follow the suggestions for individual study mentioned previously. You will find that careful preparation will greatly enrich your time spent in group discussion.

2. Be willing to participate in the discussion. The leader of your group will not be lecturing. Instead, he or she will be encouraging the members of the group to discuss what they have learned. The leader will be asking the questions that are found in this guide.

3. Stick to the topic being discussed.

4. Be sensitive to the other members of the group. Listen attentively when they describe what they have learned. You may be surprised by their insights! Many questions do not have "right" answers, particularly questions that aim at meaning or application. Instead the questions push us to explore the passage more thoroughly.

5. When possible, link what you say to the comments of others. Also be affirming whenever you can. This will encourage some of the more hesitant members of the group to participate.

6. Expect God to teach you through the passage being discussed and through the other members of the group. Pray that you will have an enjoyable and profitable time together, but also that as a result of this study, you will find ways that you can take action individually and/or as a group.

7. Remember that anything said in the group is considered confidential and should not be discussed outside the group unless specific permission is given to do so. ∎

LEADER'S GUIDE

LESSON ONE: WHERE ARE WE HEADED?

1. Begin the session with prayer. Ask God to be with you as you begin to study His Word together.

2. Play the audio segment of the CD entitled "Building a Godly Home, Part 1." Encourage group members to take notes in the section of their study guide entitled "Follow-Along Notes."

3. Begin group discussion by asking the following questions. Allow each group member ample time to answer, if they desire to do so.

   • Why is the covenant of marriage so important to God?

   • "A wedding is an event, but a marriage is an achievement." Has your own marriage been an achievement? Why or why not?

   • Think of a couple whose marriage would be considered an achievement. What are some characteristics that stand out?

4. Remind everyone to complete the "Going Deeper: Personal Study and Reflection" section for lesson two before the next group session.

5. Be sure to close in prayer. Invite the group participants to share prayer requests with the group and encourage them to pray for one another.

LESSON TWO: VIVE LA DIFFERENCE!

1. Begin the session with prayer. Ask God to be with you as you begin to study His Word together.

2. Play the audio segment of the CD entitled "Building a Godly Home, Part 2." Encourage group members to take notes in the section of their study guide entitled "Follow-Along Notes."

3. Begin group discussion by asking the following questions. Allow each group member ample time to answer, if they desire to do so.

   • What is the one thing you wish you could change about your spouse? What is the thing you would least like to change?

   • What are the "rules and regulations" of communication in your marriage? (Hint: They may be unspoken.)

   • Which are you most likely to do: look for greener grass; settle for dead grass; or create new grass? Why?

4. Remind everyone to complete the "Going Deeper: Personal Study and Reflection" section for lesson three before the next group session.

5. Be sure to close in prayer. Invite the group participants to share prayer requests with the group and encourage them to pray for one another.

LESSON THREE: RULES
FOR A HEALTHY MARRIAGE

1. Begin the session with prayer. Ask God to be with you as you begin to study His Word together.

2. Play the audio segment of the CD entitled "Building a Godly Home, Part 3." Encourage group members to take notes in the section of their study guide entitled "Follow-Along Notes."

3. Begin group discussion by asking the following questions. Allow each group member ample time to answer, if they desire to do so.

   - Describe how secrets in a marriage can become lies that erode the relationship.

   - When was the last time you used one of these phrases: "I feel as if . . ."; "Let me see if I understand"; or "I'm sorry." Describe the situation.

- If you could listen to a recording of your words from the last week, which parts would you want to edit out? Why?

4. Remind everyone to complete the "Going Deeper: Personal Study and Reflection" section for lesson four before the next group session.

5. Be sure to close in prayer. Invite the group participants to share prayer requests with the group and encourage them to pray for one another.

LESSON FOUR: THE
DYSFUNCTIONAL FAMILY REUNION

1. Begin the session with prayer. Ask God to be with you as you begin to study His Word together.

2. Play the audio segment of the CD entitled "Building a Godly Home, Part 4." Encourage group members to take notes in the section of their study guide entitled "Follow-Along Notes."

3. Begin group discussion by asking the following questions. Allow each group member ample time to answer, if they desire to do so.

   • Do you believe there is such a thing as a "functional family"? Describe the characteristics of this ideal family.

   • If you were to make up a slogan to describe your family, what would it be?

• Who are the role models from whom you learned about love, relationships, and the family? What did they teach you? How did they impact your life?

4. Be sure to close in prayer. Invite the group participants to share prayer requests with the group and encourage them to pray for one another. ■

MAX LUCADO'S

MAX on life

SERIES

AVAILABLE WHEREVER BOOKS ARE SOLD.